Come Sunday

Come
Sunday

W r i t t e n b y
Nikki Grimes
i l l u s t r a t e d b y
Michael Bryant

Eerdmans Books for Young Readers
Grand Rapids, Michigan / Cambridge, U.K.

Text © 1996 by Nikki Grimes
Illustrations © 1996 by Michael Bryant

Published 1997 by Eerdmans Books for Young Readers
an imprint of Wm. B. Eerdmans Publishing Co.
255 Jefferson Ave. S.E., Grand Rapids, Michigan 49503
P.O. Box 163, Cambridge CB3 9PU U.K.

Printed in Hong Kong

01 02 03 04 05 06 07   12 11 10 9 8 7 6

Library of Congress Cataloging-in-Publication Data

Come Sunday / by Nikki Grimes: illustrated by Michael Bryant.
p.   cm.
Summary: A little girl describes her typical Sunday from the moment her mother
wakes her up through the different elements of the worship service in church.
ISBN 0-8028-5108-8 (hardcover: alk. paper)
ISBN 0-8028-5134-7 (paperback: alk. paper)
1. Sunday — Juvenile poetry. 2. Children's poetry, American.
[1. Sunday — Poetry. 2. Afro-Americans — Poetry. 3. American poetry.]
I. Bryant, Michael, ill. II. Title.
PS3557.R489982C6 1996
811′.54 — dc20   95-33067
                               CIP
                               AC

Book design by Joy Chu

For Pierce
first, last, and always,
a child of the King —N.G.

To Pastor Jackson
and the congregation of
Bethlehem Baptist Church—
to God be the Glory —M.B.

Come Sunday

Come Sunday, Mommy wakes me up with whispers.
LaTasha, honey, she says to me.
Time to shed dawn's cozy quilt.
Come on, Sweet Pea. Open up those eyes.

I rise and wander to the kitchen,
where Mommy makes my hair and scalp
tingle with oil and comb and brush.
If only she didn't weave the braids so tight.

I fight to keep from squirming 'round
until the braiding's finally done,
'cause once I'm dressed, I look so nice,
I practically run to Paradise—
                    to Paradise Baptist Church.

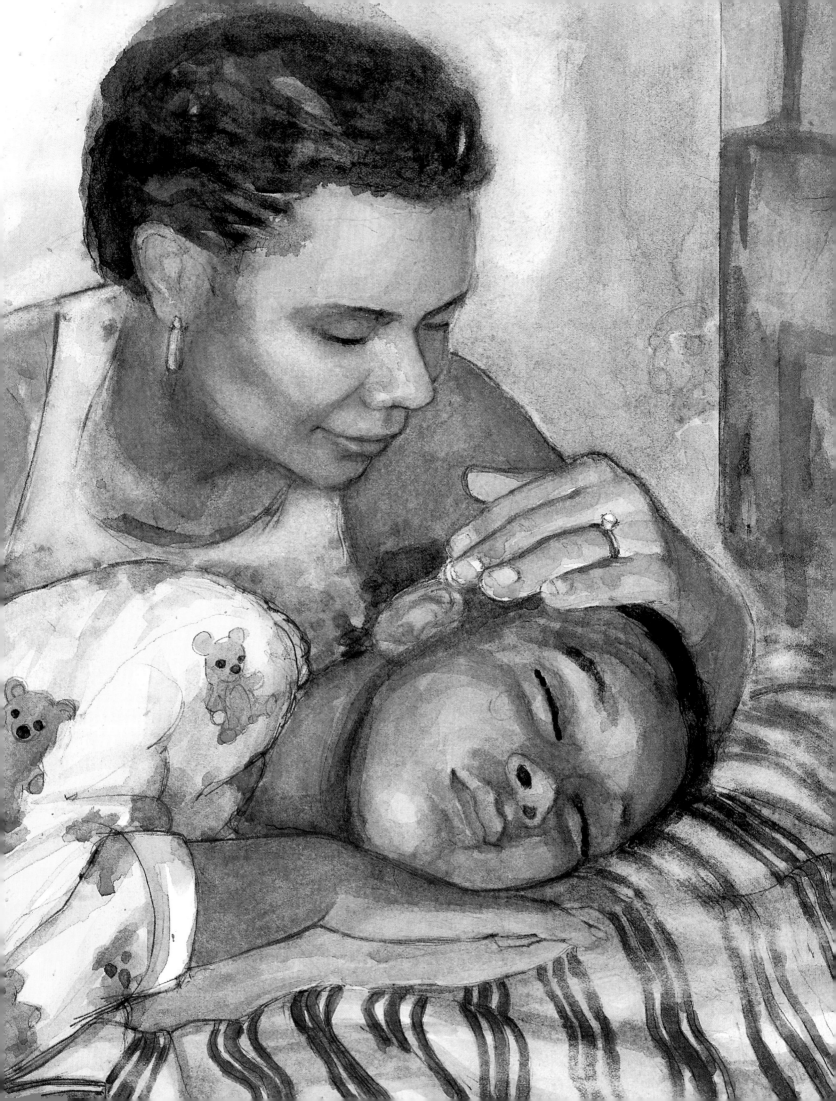

Blue-Haired Ladies

We enter the church in time to greet
the pastor's wife we sometimes meet.
I curtsy, ladylike, then see
those blue-haired ladies coming for me.
Like always, they're aching to pinch my cheek.
That's why I run from them each week.
"Come here, you precious thing," they say.
I'm itching to go the other way,
but I hold still for a minute or two,
and smile like God would want me to,
then act like there's some awful hurry
and duck into the sanctuary.

Ladies' Hats

My family settles in a pew.
I leave them for a minute or two
to race up to the balcony
and smile down on the gallery
of ladies wearing hats.

I could admire them for hours —
hats with feathers, bows, and flowers,
satin ribbons, black as jet,
broad silk bands, and lacy net
that ladies hide behind.

Some hats are peach, plum red, pale pink,
some shades of purple which I think
are beautiful, especially
on Mom, who often says that we
should dress up for the Lord.

White Gloves

I love the dazzling white gloves the ushers wear
on Communion Sunday.
And I especially love the way
Mommy's chocolatey-brown skin peeks through
the white-lace gloves she likes to wear.
And I don't care what anybody says—
next week, I'm putting on the ivory gloves
my Grandma bought for me,
the ones with ribbon threaded through.
I'll wear a matching straw hat, too,
and look just like a lady.

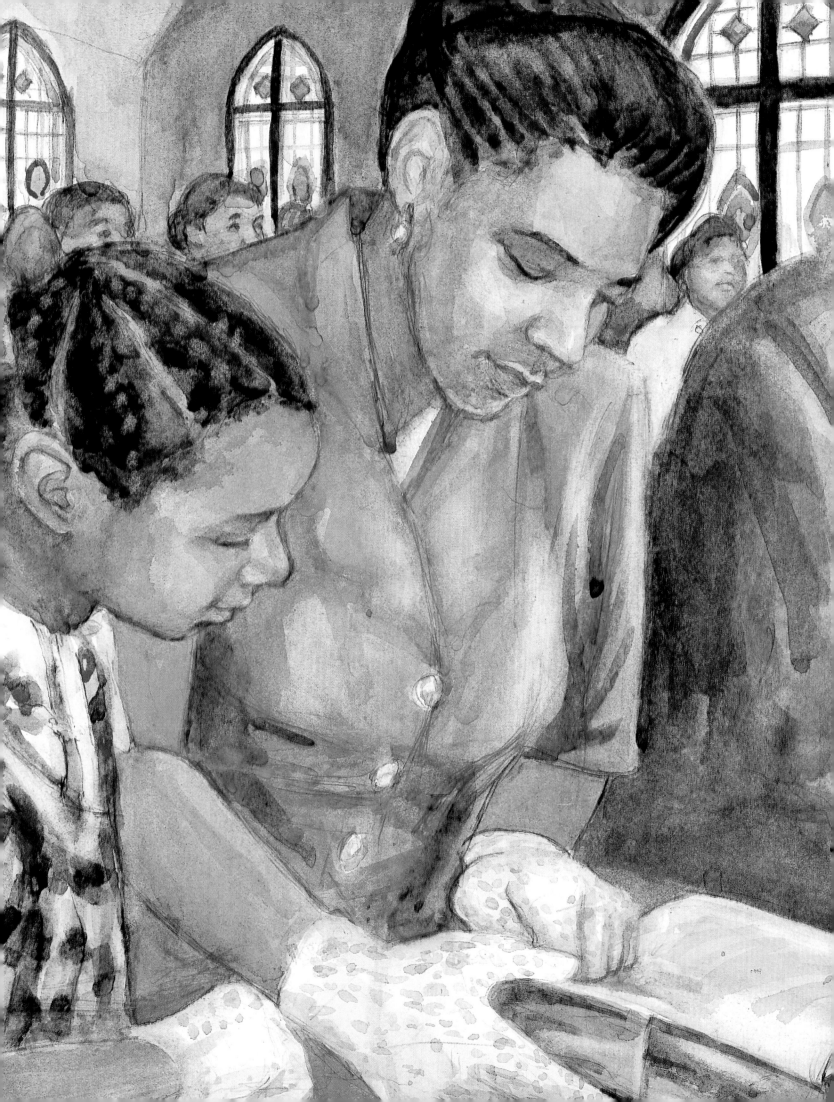

On the March

We've got walking-in music at my church,
and we clap when the ushers strut their stuff,
high-stepping down the center aisle,
their backs all straight and proud,
the Joyful Noise Choir singing loud,
"We are marching to Zion."

The drums and tambourine keep the beat,
and soon my feet are tapping up a storm.
I am march-march-marching in place,
eyes on the altar, a grin on my face.
The choir, the ushers, the pastor, and me—
we are marching to Zion together.

Jubilation

Rock-a-my-soul
 I gently sway and
Rock-a-my-soul
 I close my eyes and
Rock-a-my-soul
 I clap my hands and
Rock-a-my-soul
 my feet start dancing and
Rock-a-my-soul
 I reach for heaven and
Rock-a-my-soul
 I touch God's face and
Rock-a-my-soul
 He rocks my soul.
Oh, rock-a-my-soul.

Baptism

Down, down, down into the water,
preacher leaning over me.

Gone, gone, gone the fear of drowning,
once my father's face I see.

Up, up, up—baptized forever!
Mommy let me make the choice.

Joy, joy, joy is what I'm feeling,
hearing pride in Daddy's voice.

Esther

In Sunday School sometimes,
our teacher asks us kids
who our favorite person in the Bible is
and why. Once I raised my hand and said,
"That's easy. I like Esther,
because she's brave
and she's smart
and she's a girl—
and I'm all of that, too.
Just ask God.
He'll tell you."

My Offering

I wish we passed a basket down each row.
That way, only I would know
how many dimes I gave to God
and how many I kept for me.

Instead, we place our offering on a plate
with everybody watching, which I hate
because I'm sure they're keeping track
each time I hold some back.

Daddy says to give whatever God tells me to,
which is what I usually do—
unless I need an ice-cream cone,
and even then, if I'm alone,
I offer God a lick.

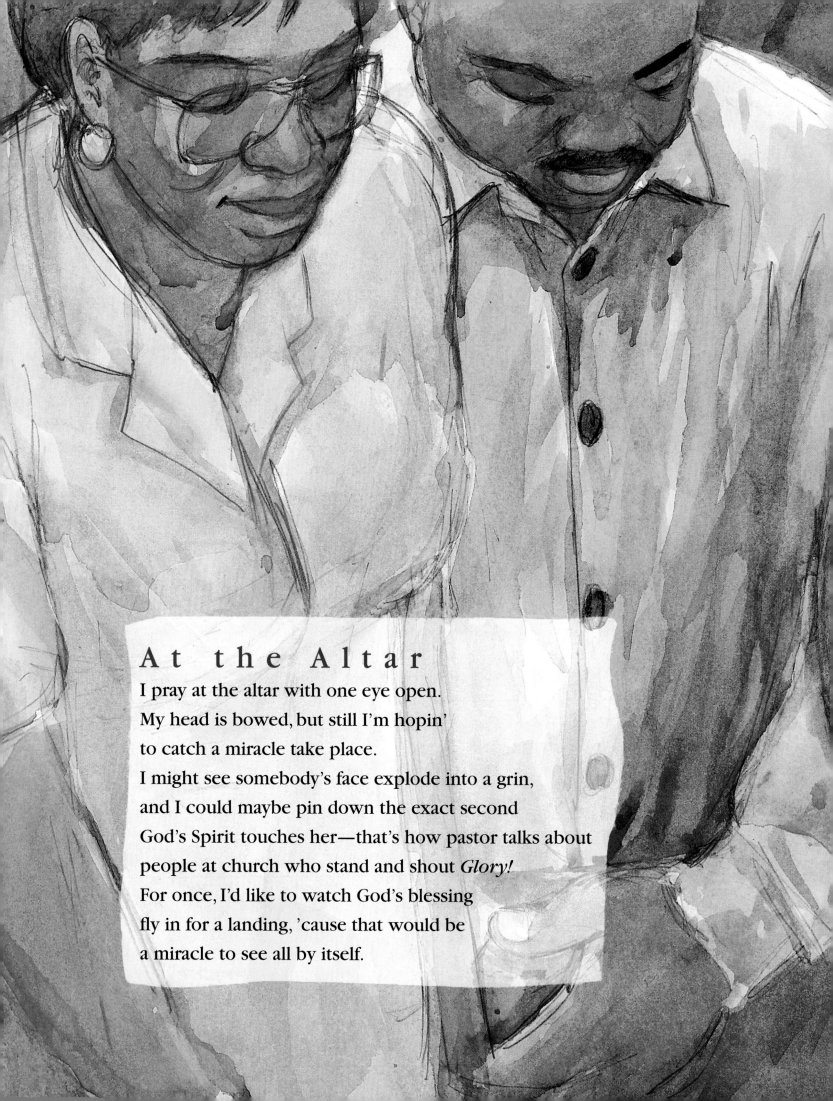

At the Altar

I pray at the altar with one eye open.
My head is bowed, but still I'm hopin'
to catch a miracle take place.
I might see somebody's face explode into a grin,
and I could maybe pin down the exact second
God's Spirit touches her—that's how pastor talks about
people at church who stand and shout *Glory!*
For once, I'd like to watch God's blessing
fly in for a landing, 'cause that would be
a miracle to see all by itself.

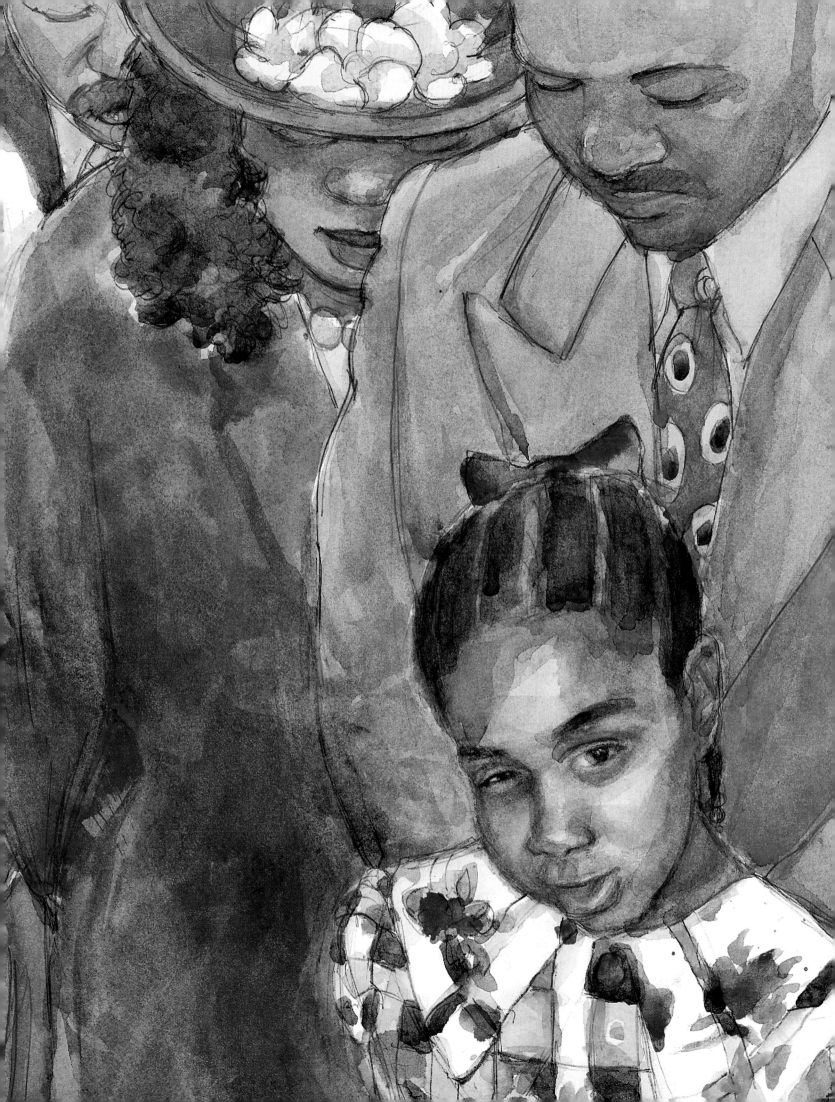

Church Supper

Sundays and church suppers go together,
even better than collards and ham
and honey-glazed yams,
fried chicken and black-eyed peas,
and pumpkin pie—and I better stop
before my stomach starts to growl.

While pastor preaches,
I can't help but wiggle in my pew.
Some Sundays, it's all I can do
to keep from crisscrossing the floor
and tearing through the door
that leads to the church dining hall.

I check the clock (it's way past noon)
and pray that the service will be over soon,
and sometimes, when it is,
I yell "Amen" louder than anyone there,
and hardly care who hears me,
'cause all I can think about is food!

Lady Preacher

Sunday afternoons mean visiting preachers,
spirit-filled teachers like Sister Beverly,
who usually speaks soft and low just so
we all have to lean in close to hear.
The Holy One has a word for us today,
children, she'll say, and right away
I feel a shiver go up my spine, 'cause I'm
pretty sure it's God who's doing the talking,
and not just Sister Beverly. The whole church
knows it too, 'cause when she preaches,
even our pastor has to say *Amen, Sister!*
Praise the Lord!

Sunday Evening

Come Sunday evening, I always know,
without being told, when it's time to go:
the deacons begin gathering fans from each pew,
then check underneath, where they find one or two;
my tummy starts growling for supper once more,
and right about then, Mommy strolls toward the door;
then I take Daddy's hand, and the last thing I hear
is the hum of the organ whispering soft in my ear,
and the melody follows me home.

Lights Out

"Now I lay me down to sleep,
I ask the Lord my soul to keep,"
I pray before I crawl in bed.
Mommy tucks me in. I shake my head,
still wondering where the long day went,
although I'm glad I spent
another day in Paradise.